SHIRE ARCHAEC

D1339971

2

Cover photograph
An aerial view of the pewter-manufacturing village site of
Little Down, on the Lansdown plateau near Bath, Avon.
(Photograph courtesy of Mick Aston.)

British Library Cataloguing in Publication Data available

Published by
SHIRE PUBLICATIONS LTD
Cromwell House, Church Street, Princes Risborough,
Aylesbury, Bucks HP17 9AJ, UK.

Series Editor: James Dyer

ISBN 0 85263 875 2.

First published 1987

Set in 11 point Times and printed in Great Britain by
C. I. Thomas & Sons (Haverfordwest) Ltd,
Press Buildings, Merlins Bridge, Haverfordwest, Dyfed

Contents

4

List of illustrations

Acknowledgements

I am grateful to the following people for their various contributions to the writing of this book: James Dyer, Series Editor, for reading and approving the initial precis; Jeffrey May, Andrew Poulter and Colin Pendleton, for much helpful advice on the preparation of the typescript and for continuous interest in the project; Sarah Lucy, for the production of the excellent artistic reconstruction; and Bernard Rawes for photographs and for much helpful information about his sites in Gloucestershire. T. Potter of the British Museum kindly allowed me to use an unpublished photograph of his Stonea excavations and Simon Palmer, of the Oxfordshire Archaeological Unit, was most helpful in the provision of information, plans and photographs of the unit's work at Claydon Pike. Richard Kent allowed me to use unpublished plans from his work at Little Down and Derrick Riley was very helpful concerning aerial photographs of Dunstan's Clump.

Permission for the use of other illustrations was given by B. Cunliffe, M. Todd, A. Detsicas, the Royal Commission on Historical Monuments, R. Leech, W. J. Wedlake, G. Jobey, the Chelmsford Archaeological Trust, the Somerset Archaeological Society and Professor P. Fowler, who also viewed the typescript. David Wilson, of the Committee for Aerial Photography at Cambridge, was very helpful in the provision of aerial photographs.

I would like to thank Janet Murray for the loan of drawing equipment and for compiling the index, and also my mother, who demonstrated continual interest in the progress of the book and aided me in my fieldwork on the Roman sites of Lansdown. This book is dedicated to the memory of my father, Keith Thomas Hanley.

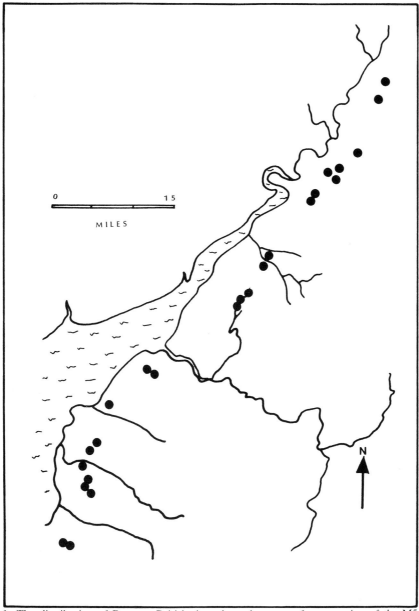

1. The distribution of Romano-British sites along the route of construction of the M5 motorway. (After Fowler.)

1
Introduction

The study of villages in Roman Britain has come of age only in comparatively recent years, for until the 1960s Roman archaeologists tended to concentrate upon the materially reward-ing sites of villas, towns and forts. Indeed, after the Second World War, the existence of village-type settlements within the Romano-British countryside was placed in doubt, it being suggested instead that the sole units of rural settlement were the Romanised villa estate and the poor native farmstead consisting of a few farm buildings. In 1964 an important article was published in the *Antiquaries Journal* by S. J. Hallam in which the case for the presence of Roman villages in the archaeological record was restated, although at that time they were referred to as 'nucleated settlements'. In subsequent years there has been a dramatic increase in interest in the archaeology of the countryside and Romano-British village settlements are now viewed as being widespread. Some archaeologists have even suggested that in terms of village numbers the Roman rural landscape was very similar to that of the medieval period. Support for this view of dense settlement came from the excavations carried out in advance of motorway building, as in the case of the M5, where Roman rural settlements were observed in very close proximity to each other (figure 1).

The term 'village' is not frequently used in academic circles, where such descriptions as 'native settlements' or 'rural settle-ments' are preferred, because it is often difficult to assign modern terminology to Romano-British settlement. The term is useful, however, in the context of this book in that it enables the examination of a wide variety of settlement types to take place under one rather elastic heading. 'Village' encompasses all the different types of settlement which fall outside the categories of either single-family farmsteads or urban centres — the towns of Roman Britain. Included within this broad spectrum are the small hamlets of Cornwall and the northern frontier, as well as the larger lowland settlements such as the 'small towns', where substantial concentrations of population were centred on the Roman road system.

2
Iron age to Roman Britain

The study of villages in iron age Britain has been as neglected as the study of those of the Roman period. Until the late 1930s it was believed that in the lowland areas iron age man lived in 'pit dwellings', although such squalid pits were totally incompatible with the constructional achievements of the period, exemplified in the larger hillforts of southern Britain. It was not until 1938 that the existence of the lowland iron age settlement of the type familiar today was established in the excavations carried out at the site of Little Woodbury, Wiltshire, by the German archaeologist G. Bersu. By the use of new archaeological techniques Bersu demonstrated that the 'pit dwellings' were storage pits and that, rather than living in holes in the ground, iron age man inhabited timber roundhouses. A similar site has since been excavated at Gussage All Saints, Dorset, where a village dated by pottery to the period between the fourth century BC and the first century AD was discovered, with evidence for pit storage and metalworking. Another site of this type was uncovered at Walesland Rath, Dyfed, revealing a number of circular wooden huts set within a concentric banked enclosure. Some of the hillforts of the iron age also contained large village-type communities, as in the case of such excavated examples as Maiden Castle in Dorset, Crickley Hill in Gloucestershire and Moel y Gaer in Clwyd.

In highland areas stone-built roundhouses were commonplace in the iron age, as seen for example at the long-occupied site of Jarlshof, Shetland, and at Bodrifty in Cornwall. Cornwall also yields evidence for an alternative settlement type in the form of the distinctive 'rounds' and these will be examined in chapter 3, because they often demonstrate continuity from the iron age into the Romano-British period.

The site of Dragonby, Humberside (figure 2), provides a good example of a large and highly prosperous iron age settlement, with evidence for trading links with continental Europe. In the iron age the site consisted of a number of circular timber huts and rectangular enclosures but in the Roman period these were replaced by the characteristically Romano-British rectangular stone buildings, which were aligned end-on to a metalled road, set back within individual ditched enclosures. The typical building type in the lowlands during the iron age was the circular

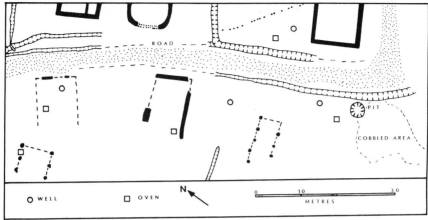

2. The Romano-British phase at Dragonby, Humberside, with buildings of both stone and timber construction set inside ditched enclosures beside the main road. (After May.)

3. The site of Butcombe, Avon. 'A' is the only excavated building. (After Fowler.)

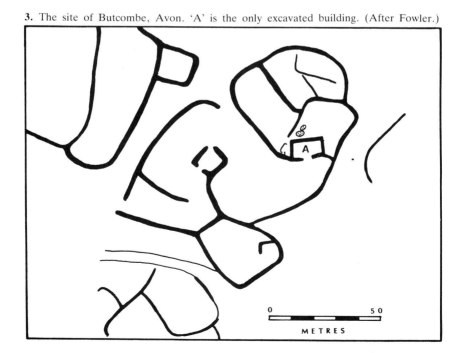

4. Cropmarks in the parishes of Lechlade and Fairford, Gloucestershire. (Photograph: University of Cambridge copyright reserved.)

timber hut, usually constructed from either a single or a double post ring, but this form was widely replaced in the Roman period by rectangular buildings and these rapidly became the norm in the centuries following the Roman conquest of Britain, although some examples of rectangular buildings are known from the iron age, as at the hillfort site of Crickley Hill. Settlements similar to Dragonby are known from elsewhere in Britain and at the sites of Baldock and Braughing in Hertfordshire such settlements lie in proximity to later Roman 'small towns'.

Like Braughing and Baldock, a number of villages demonstrate continuity from the iron age. It will be seen later that this is particularly true in the case of highland areas, although instances are well known from the lowlands, as at Butcombe in Avon (figure 3) and Chalton, Hampshire. Of about 140 village sites identified by the author in the area of Avon, Somerset and Gloucestershire, 36 sites provided definite proof of iron age activity, with it being suspected at many more. It is clear that the vast bulk of the population of all Romano-British villages was derived from the native iron age communities. There was no influx of new people, just a change in the form of the villages themselves. The population remained largely static.

The intensive utilisation of the land in both the iron age and Roman periods is known from the work carried out at such complex sites as those found on the upper Thames at Lechlade and Fairford, in Gloucestershire, seen best from the air (figure 4). This area provides a good example of what can be achieved by a concentrated excavation over a considerable area. The observed remains included drainage ditches, building and enclosure indications, sunken roads and field systems. Subsequent excavations carried out at one of these sites, that at Claydon Pike, revealed a sizable settlement with an organised street plan and with stone and timber houses. Work of a similar nature has been carried out at Dunstan's Clump in Nottinghamshire (figures 20 and 21). Such a programme of intensive survey and selective excavation is potentially of great value to the study of Roman rural archaeology. This is also the case with regional studies, which are necessary if the density and type of rural settlement within any area are to be fully appreciated.

3
Villages in highland areas

In the highland areas of Britain the Roman conquest was to have only a limited effect upon the indigenous native communities, which were already organised into small nucleated village societies. The economy of the villages in these regions was primarily pastoral and exhibited many more traits of iron age culture than of Roman. In part, this continuity of iron age identity was due to the fact that most highland areas lay in Roman military zones. Even in those parts where the army had departed, continued hostility towards Roman culture combined with the inherent poverty of these areas resulted in a very noticeable lack of the traits of Romanisation in the settlements. This is especially apparent when such villages are compared to their lowland counterparts. Another reason for the failure of the normally successful force of Romanisation can be attributed to the inaccessibility of the highlands, which lacked the advanced road systems found in other parts of the province.

The resulting cultural isolation of the highlands is well illustrated by the widespread continuation of the iron age house form and settlement plan. Good examples of this can be seen in the plans of the sites excavated at Greaves Ash and Southernknowe (figures 5 and 6) on the northern frontier, with their concentric enclosures and circular stone huts. Villas and urban centres are absent from highland areas, as was the marketing potential that they offered to native rural communities. It appears that the local native aristocracy was either too poor or too proud to build villas and investment from outside would be unlikely, because of the unprofitability of the highlands. In Cornwall there is only one known villa site, at Magor, and in the north the few villas that existed are all to be found to the south of Hadrian's Wall and outside the extensive zone of military control, from which villa settlements appear to have been excluded. The only centres of Romanisation on the whole frontier were the fortside villages *(vici)* as found at Housesteads and *Vindolanda* (figure 7) and these were primarily involved in the life of the nearby fort.

The extent of upland occupation in Britain during the Roman period is a very wide subject, and therefore the rest of this chapter will examine two example areas, the northern frontier and Cornwall.

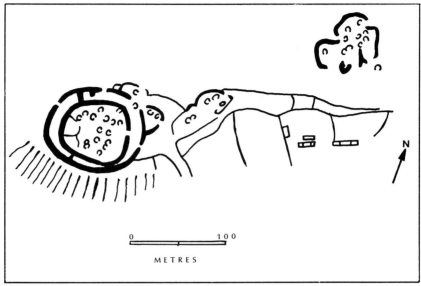

5. The large settlement at Greaves Ash, Northumberland. (After Jobey.)

The northern frontier

This region includes the land lying both to the north and to the south of Hadrian's Wall in northern England and southern Scotland. Within this area the work of Professor G. Jobey has been of great value, for it was largely as a result of his efforts that many of the sites referred to were both identified and excavated. Settlements to the north of Hadrian's Wall are included because in the second century much of southern Scotland up to the Forth and Clyde rivers was incorporated into the province of Britain, following the advances that led to the construction of the Antonine Wall. The territory of the tribe called the Votadini, centred in south-east Scotland around the tribal capital of Traprain Law, Lothian, has produced numerous village remains from this period.

Most villages on the northern frontier were small, normally of little more than an acre (0.4 ha) in size, defined by a boundary stockade or wall which normally enclosed four to five round huts of iron age type. They appear to have been pastorally based, although most yielded some evidence for limited arable cultivation and in the coastal plains and lowland valleys quite extensive agriculture would have been possible. The villages, although

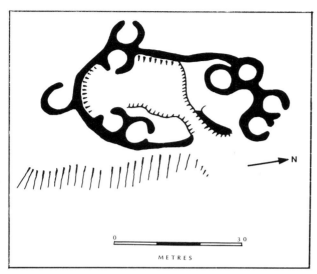

N

0   30

METRES

enclosed, were non-defensive in nature and the palisade, wall or
bank which normally surrounded the hut group was probably
intended merely to keep out wild animals and to provide a secure
stockade in which livestock could be sheltered. Typical settlements of this type can be seen between the rivers Tyne and Forth,
where enclosed villages of round stone-built huts were the norm.
Such sites are often seen to lie in a pre-Roman context and in
Northumberland a number were located close to prehistoric
hillforts. Groups of simple circular huts fronting on to a central
courtyard or 'scooped' court were very common within the
frontier area in both the iron age and Roman periods and a
number of these sites demonstrate continuity from the iron age,
especially in the more hilly areas.

   The reuse of previously deserted prehistoric settlement sites is
also attested, as at Huckhoe in Northumberland. This settlement
yielded evidence for iron age occupation in the sixth century BC,
with the later phase being dated to the second century AD
onwards and apparently lasting well into the early medieval
period. Huckhoe may be regarded as a fairly typical example of a
'courtyard' village, with an enclosure wall surrounding round
stone-built houses. At Southernknowe some of the houses were
built into the enclosure wall and it is possible to identify separate
units within the settlement plan (figure 6). Villages of this type
are commonplace in the region between the second and fourth

centuries AD, for example in the Cheviot foothills. A very large example of such a village has been excavated at Greaves Ash, Northumberland (figure 5), which can also be seen in the context of its surrounding field systems, implying some degree of arable cultivation. The 'scooped' enclosures, so called due to their sunken courtyards as seen at the site of Coldsmouth Hill, may well have been the forerunners of the Huckhoe village 'type' and their scooped appearance may possibly have arisen from the presence of large numbers of livestock within the compound as well as from the need for spoil for the construction of the enclosure circuit. These villages might possess either stone or timber round huts.

To the south of the Roman military road which ran to the important outpost fort at High Rochester, north of Hadrian's Wall, a number of settlements of rectangular rather than concentric form have been identified. This rectangular form suggests a level of Roman influence as it is common to many Roman sites. Villages like Birtley possessed the standard four or five huts, which fronted on to cobbled yards and are normally of the first or second century in date. Jobey suggested that villages with this rectangular form might represent Roman imperial development of the area immediately to the north of Hadrian's Wall, in an attempt to civilise the frontier region, thereby reducing the constant threat of hostility against the frontier line and providing a Romanised buffer between the province and the fierce Caledonian tribes to the north. This argument is supported by the observation of over forty such villages within 20 miles (32 km) of the frontier line. Other rectilinear settlements are found elsewhere in the frontier area, but are limited mainly to low-lying locations. They usually consist of round stone-built houses with cobbled yards, again suggesting a pastoral economy. In the north Tyne valley, excavated rectilinear enclosures have demonstrated the replacement of iron age type wooden huts and palisades by stone houses and enclosing walls in the second century AD.

The accumulated evidence from all of these frontier sites seems to suggest that in the second century AD there was a considerable expansion and development of village-type settlements within the region, and this appears to be at least partly associated with direct Roman political intervention, apparently aimed at stabilising the potentially hostile native communities of the north.

Evidence for the economy of these villages comes from a number of sites. It seems to indicate that the rural economy within the region was highly localised and insular, with the exception of the large settlements beside forts. At Riding Wood and other sites the frequent finds of spindle whorls provide evidence for weaving, thereby indicating the role of sheep in the village economy. Small-scale metalworking is also known, as in the finds of slag deposits made during the excavation of Huckhoe. The primarily pastoral nature of these settlements is clear, however, with the bones of sheep and cattle being frequently found. The presence of yards and enclosures also testifies that the keeping of livestock constituted a vital part of the village economy. As has been previously stated, limited crop cultivation is also suggested at a number of sites. It is often indicated by the finding of quern stones, used for grinding the corn into flour. A number of villages have their fields surviving nearby, as can be seen at Greaves Ash (figure 5). The study of the plant pollen remains from this area in the Roman period suggests that widespread forest clearances were taking place, thereby increasing the amount of available agricultural land, and presumably indicating an increase in the population of the area, based on the

7. The fort and *vicus* at Chesterholm *(Vindolanda)* on Hadrian's Wall. (Photograph: University of Cambridge copyright reserved.)

villages. The simple rural economy of these sites appears to have been flourishing during the Roman period.

A final group of settlements in the north is the fortside villages *(vici)* of the frontier zone, the best known examples of which are the extensively excavated sites at Housesteads and at *Vindolanda* on Hadrian's Wall (figure 7). Although these sites are considerably larger than any 'native' settlements in the north, it is still possible to view them as villages, comparable to the 'small towns' of southern Britain (see chapter 6). They were sited outside the forts and they served the needs of the garrison, as well as providing a home for the soldiers' families. These sites had an important marketing function for both the fort and the local area and this is apparent in the presence of suggested shops within many of these settlements, which were often also centres of industrial production and manufacturing. Agriculture was also of considerable relevance to the inhabitants of these *vici*, as at Housesteads, where aerial photographs reveal the presence of a number of field terraces close to the settlement, which was probably self-sufficient in terms of arable production. These *vici* also provided a number of alternative services. At Housesteads, for example, there was a temple and at *Vindolanda* there was a large official posting station *(mansio)*.

Cornwall

In the far south-west of Britain lay the tribal territory of Dumnonia, one of the poorest regions within the province. It appears also to have been one of the areas least affected by the arrival of both Roman administration and 'civilisation' and it therefore demonstrates a far greater level of iron age continuity than many other highland areas. As in the north, this continuity of iron age traditions can be attributed to the lack of Romanising influences within Dumnonia, a state of affairs convincingly demonstrated by the identification of only one villa site within the whole Cornish peninsula. The nearest Roman town was at Exeter, which developed out of the fort on that site in the late first century, but the existence of Roman authority within the region is attested archaeologically in the site of the small fort at Nanstallon and is also inferred from the finds of Roman milestones, which suggests imperial involvement in Dumnonian territory. This involvement may well have been due to the abundance of the valuable tin reserves found in Cornwall, an asset mentioned by Roman historians. It has been long suspected that an ancient tin trade existed between Cornwall and the

8. A typical Cornish round associated with a hillfort at Tregonning Hill. (Photograph: University of Cambridge copyright reserved.)

continent and some parts of the region appear to demonstrate greater compatibility with continental cultures than with British ones.

The Cornish tin mines probably reached their productive peak during the third and fourth centuries AD, as in this period the supply of imported metal from other provinces dwindled. The main demand for the ore came from the manufacturers of pewter, who were themselves filling a gap in the market for fine tablewares, brought about by the exhaustion of the Spanish silver mines and their associated fineware industries. It seems likely that, as at the Mendip lead mines, villages would have grown up at the main tin extraction sites in order to house the workers, whether or not the mines were worked under direct imperial control. Although no such sites have been found, their existence is likely, but detection would be very difficult because of the effects of successive mining operations upon the remains, as has been observed at the lead-mining settlement at Charterhouse-on-Mendip.

In its lack of villas and towns and in the unromanised nature of the native village settlements Cornwall shared a feature with the northern frontiers. Unlike the north, however, the region could not even reap the acculturising benefits of being within a long-standing military zone and it therefore lacked the economic stimulus which the presence of the army could provide and which in the north led to the development of the fortside *vici*. In every sense Dumnonia was both a political and a cultural backwater as far as the Roman administration would have been concerned. Even the fort at Nanstallon was occupied for only a short period of time.

The types of village settlement found within the region substantiate this conclusion. It is very difficult to separate archaeologically the iron age and Roman periods because of the apparently unaltered continuation of the standard village forms. The best example of this continuity can be seen in the highly distinctive Cornish 'rounds' (figure 8). This type of settlement appears to be iron age in origin but a number of examples were constructed after the Roman conquest. Rounds are basically univallate enclosures possessing a single bank and ditch which enclosed the site area and are normally of concentric form. As in the north, these circuits were of an essentially non-defensive nature. Within the general round category there is a great variety of forms. Some sites could be very large, like those at Carvossa and Trevisker. At the latter there was apparently a dramatic increase in the size of the settlement, possibly due to a substantial population increase. Some other rounds possess curious annexes of indeterminate function but which may be corralling areas because, as in the north, these settlements were probably primarily pastoral in nature.

An alternative type of village settlement is apparent in the higher country at the site of Chysauster. This village demonstrates continuity from the iron age, dating from the first century BC to the first century AD. The site was constructed from the simple rubble-built bank, with the rooms of the separate houses being located within the enclosure wall, all fronting on to the typical central courtyard. The site is therefore similar in organisation to the northern frontier village at Southernknowe (figure 6). As in the north, some of the Cornish villages can be viewed in the context of their own field systems and it is possible that some of the unassociated field complexes known in the region might belong to as yet unidentified open village settlements.

A final form of rural occupation in Dumnonia was that which was located inside the purely iron age hillfort sites, as at Castle Dore, although it is likely that the occupation of heavily defended sites such as hillforts would have been quickly discouraged by the Roman administration.

4
Smaller lowland villages

The villages in this category demonstrate a considerable level of Roman influence, in contrast to those settlements examined in the previous chapter. This is primarily due to their more amenable lowland position and consequent contact with direct Roman influence. The attributes of Romanisation found within such villages include such things as building form and construction, settlement layout and new agricultural techniques, like well sinking. Roman influence is also very apparent in the kinds of finds made during the excavation of such sites, where in normal circumstances a number of Roman coins would be expected. Such coins demonstrate the presence, in some form, of a monetary economy, thereby indicating contact between the village and the outside world. As well as money, excavators might expect to find other Romanised trappings, such as fine objects of bronze, including brooches, rings, pins and cosmetic items, alongside technologically advanced iron tools. Fine pottery wares would also be found on most sites, in the form of samian, the fine pottery imported to Britain in the first and second centuries. In the later Roman period other finewares appear in greater profusion, such as the third- and fourth-century AD products of the Oxford, Nene Valley and New Forest pottery industries, which were producing high-quality grinding bowls (*mortaria*) and richly slipped tablewares.

Despite such semblances of Romanisation, however, these villages were primarily agriculturally based, located off major routes of communication and essentially insular and localised in terms of their marketing and other economic activities.

Buildings

The most apparent feature of Romanisation visible in these villages was their widespread use of the rectangular house plan, well known archaeologically from such sites as Dragonby (Humberside, figure 2), Chalton (Hampshire) and Butcombe in Avon (figure 3). In Sussex and Hampshire this adoption appears to have taken place widely in the second century AD and a similar course of development is visible in many other areas. As in the north, the rectangular building form tended to replace the traditional iron age roundhouse, for example at Butcombe, where a second-century rectangular structure replaced a round

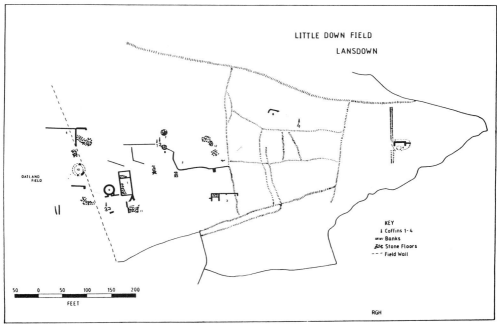

9. The industrial settlement of Little Down on Lansdown, near Bath, where there were a number of suggested buildings. (After Bush, Kent and Hanley.)

hut of iron age date. During the first two centuries AD such rectangular buildings consisted of a timber superstructure, set either on to a narrow sill wall or into a wooden beam laid in a shallow trench on the ground. Such sill beams are normally fairly easy to discern during excavation because of the presence of the beam slot, which normally survives if the ground conditions allow. Sill walls are less easy to identify, as it is sometimes difficult to tell whether or not the excavated wall was of sill type or merely the remains of the lower courses of a wall which reached up to the eaves of the building. Much depends on the interpretation of the thickness and construction of the wall.

Excavations in Somerset at Catsgore and the 'small town' of Ilchester have revealed the plans of a number of early timber-framed buildings. As is suggested by the term 'timber-framed', the superstructure of buildings such as these was of timber, frequently used in association with such traditional building materials as wattle and daub, with wall plaster also often being found. Such buildings have been excavated within a number of Roman towns, as at *Verulamium* (St Albans) and in Kent, where some of the farmsteads of that region possessed timber-framed walls based on stone sills.

A problem encountered in the excavation of both rural and urban sites is the destruction of the earlier Roman levels in which such timber buildings are usually found by later levels, where stone building was normal. The stone rectangular form became commonplace in the third and fourth centuries AD, with many examples being known, as at Little Down, Avon (figure 9), and from even earlier periods at Dragonby, Humberside (figure 2). Their uses were very varied, some no doubt being dwellings whilst others might have been storage places or workshops. At Little Down, where such buildings were used in the industrial production of both pewter and iron, they were often well constructed with dressed and mortared blocks and the roofs were commonly of the typical Roman stone tiles, with their distinctive nail holes (see figure 39). Thatch was probably another popular roofing material and its presence has been suggested at the large site of Chelmsford and is presumably to be expected at these smaller sites. Clay tiles appear to have been used in a number of instances, although they were likely to have been fairly expensive and reserved for the more affluent members of the village community.

The use of mud as a building material in some areas should not be ruled out, for in the medieval period 'mud and stud' buildings were comparatively common in such counties as Nottinghamshire and Lincolnshire. Their archaeological remains would be tenuous at best.

Occasionally these village buildings, although unpretentious in plan, could aspire to some level of luxury, as at the small village site at Park Brow in Sussex, where the timber, wattle and daub houses possessed glazed windows. Such glazing is a sure sign of some affluence and this impression is strengthened by the finding of a door key at the same site, indicating that the contents of the houses at Park Brow were of sufficient value to require door locks.

Although the rectangular building plan became the normal type in lowland Britain in the Roman period, the circular form did not disappear altogether and a number of lowland sites yield evidence for the continued use of wooden circular huts of iron age type. The sites associated with such buildings tended to be poor as at the first- and second-century AD site at East Tilbury in Essex, where four circular huts built out of timber, wattle and daub were excavated. Similar structures were uncovered at Green Ore on Mendip, a site engaged in the extraction of silver from the locally mined lead ore. Better appointed roundhouses

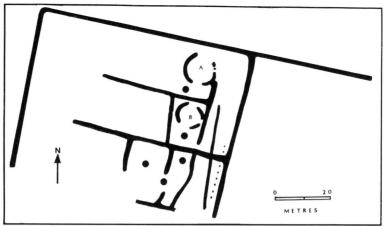

10. Brockworth, Gloucestershire. 'A' and 'B' are the Roman-period circular buildings. The dots represent the site of other later buildings, which appear to have been set in rectangular plots. A line of fence posts runs inside one of the regular boundary ditches. (After Rawes.)

have been discovered at the site of Brockworth, close to the Roman *colonia* town at Gloucester (figures 10 and 12). At that site excavations revealed two eavesdrip gullies, designed to remove rainwater as it fell from the probably thatched roof, thereby preventing the ground around the hut from becoming saturated. The Brockworth buildings lasted into the second century, when they appear to have been replaced by rectangular timber structures. Circular stone buildings of indeterminate function are also known from Little Down, Avon (figure 9).

Some of these villages possessed small wayside shrines of Roman type which were presumably constructed to house Roman or Romano-Celtic gods, indicating the adoption of foreign deities within the rural communities. At the Portway site, also close to Gloucester, a polygonal temple was excavated close to a podium which probably marked the site of another religious building (figure 14). A carved stone head was found nearby. Two temples were also suggested at the site of Claydon Pike, on the upper Thames on the Oxfordshire border (figure 15). Excavations on this site revealed a standard Roman-type square temple as well as a smaller circular stone example.

An aisled building of a form commonly seen in the agricultural areas of villas was also found at Claydon Pike and was presumably associated with the storage of grain. The plan of the site suggests the existence of a rudimentary street plan, with the main street or hollow way approaching and running through the village, with lanes branching off at right angles to it. A similar street grid has been suggested for the village at Chisenbury Warren, Wiltshire, and also at Dragonby, Humberside. At the Portway site (figure 13) there appears to have been a cobbled

11. One of the circular houses at Brockworth, Gloucestershire. (Photograph: B. Rawes.)

lane leading from the rutted main road of the Roman period towards the polygonal temple (figure 19).

Settlement economy

These villages were primarily agricultural in terms of their economic base, with the villagers being closely bound to the land. This vital agricultural basis for the existence of the settlements is

12. The settlement enclosure ditch at Brockworth, Gloucestershire. Note the line of fence posts (Photograph: B. Rawes.)

13. The Portway, Gloucestershire. 'S' marks the location of the two suggested shrines. The dots mark the location of rectangular buildings. Note the areas of cobbling leading off the main road. (After Rawes.)

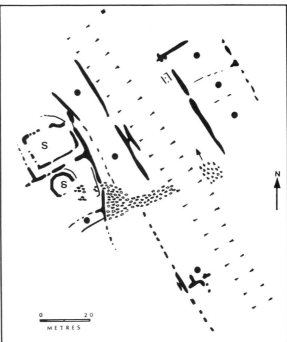

0   20
METRES

14. The polygonal shrine at Portway, Gloucestershire. (Photograph: B. Rawes.)

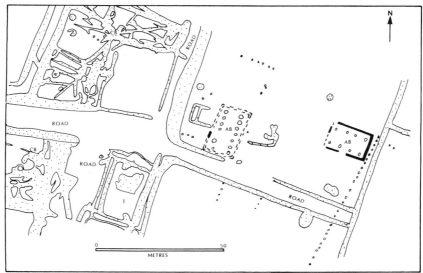

15. Claydon Pike, on the Gloucestershire-Oxfordshire border. 'CB' signifies a cottage-type building and 'AB' represents an aisled barn. 'T' marks the site of the suggested temple. (Oxford Archaeological Unit.)

apparent in the frequency with which they can be seen to lie in the context of their surrounding fields. These fields and the drove-ways that linked them have been traced in a number of cases by the use of aerial photography, which shows the cultivation lynchets and field boundaries far more clearly than any ground-level survey could. A good example of the results which can be obtained from the air is the work of Derrick N. Riley in his identification of the so-called 'brickwork' field systems of north

16. The early Roman temple at Claydon Pike. (Photograph: Oxford Archaeological Unit.)

17. The early Roman aisled barn at Claydon Pike. (Photograph: Oxford Archaeological Unit.)

Nottinghamshire. This work led to the excavation of the small Romano-British settlement site of Dunstan's Clump (figures 20 and 21).

The typical field unit in the Romano-British rural landscape was the misleadingly titled 'Celtic field', so named because the fields of this type were originally thought to be iron age in date, although their origins have since been proved to be much more ancient. These plots tend to be approximately square, in contrast to the Roman-style rectangular strip field, demonstrating that the majority of settlements probably either maintained pre-existing

18. General view of the excavations at Claydon Pike, showing the later Roman farm which succeeded the central part of the village. (Photograph: Oxford Archaeological Unit.)

19. The cart-rutted cobbled roadway at Portway, Gloucestershire. (Photograph: B. Rawes.)

prehistoric fields or laid out new ones in the traditional manner. The difference between the two field types is demonstrated at the village site of Butcombe in Avon. The excavator, Peter Fowler, observed the presence of Celtic fields around both the excavated site and the nearby and contemporary site of Scars Farm. To the south of these, however, around the villa site at Lye's Hole, the fields appear to be of the Romanised strip type (figure 22). It was suggested that this situation might represent the independence of the native villages from the Roman villa, whose owner was practising the new imported agricultural techniques.

Fields associated with villages can be quoted in a number of instances. At Chalton, Hampshire, a sizable settlement, visible in the earthworks of its rectangular houses, was surrounded by a large complex of field boundaries. As this site was occupied in the late iron age it is possible that its field system originated in that period. Such might also be the case at Thundersbarrow Hill in the territory of the Regni (modern Sussex and Hampshire), where an extensive field system can be traced around the village, which lies below an iron age hillfort (figure 23). The Park Brow settlement in Sussex can also be seen in its agricultural surroundings of fields and droveways. Claydon Pike, on the upper Thames, is another site with numerous field remains in its vicinity, with large numbers of fields and lanes being indicated by aerial photo-

20. Dunstan's Clump, Nottinghamshire. (Photograph: D. Riley.)

graphs. These show that the whole locality is covered by a dense network of nucleated village settlements and fields (figure 4). Similar complex field systems have been observed in Wiltshire, at the Totterdown and Overton Down sites, and in Gloucestershire ditched field boundaries have been excavated at the villages of Brockworth and Portway (figures 10 and 13).

Dorset and the southern downlands provide good evidence for intensive settlement in the Roman period, with a mass of small settlements linked by trackways, which formed the focus for village development. Some of the villages reached a considerable

21. Dunstan's Clump, Nottinghamshire. View of the site. (Photograph: D. Riley.)

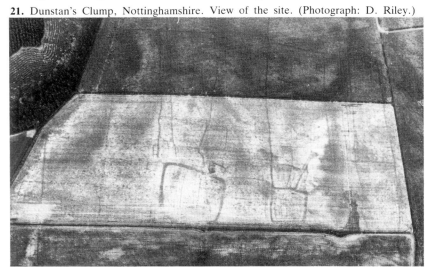

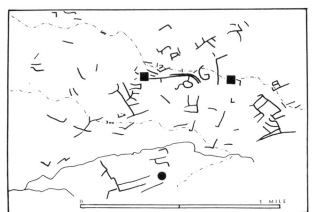

22. The fields in the vicinity of the villages of Butcombe and Scars Farm (shown by squares) and the villa at Lye's Hole, Avon (shown by dot). (After Fowler.)

size, as at Chisenbury Warren, Wiltshire, and similarly large sites are known elsewhere, such as the 17 acre (7 ha) settlement at Chalton, Hampshire, and the 15 acre (6 ha) site at Bulphan in Essex. Nevertheless, in terms of their Romanisation they remained essentially poor and therefore bound to the land like their smaller counterparts. Many of these smaller villages appear to succeed iron age occupation of the same site, as has already been seen at Thundersbarrow Hill (figure 23) and Chalton. Such was also the case at the villages of Woodcuts (Dorset), Claydon Pike and Dragonby. Dragonby had been a very important iron age site in the east Midlands but appears to have entered a decline in the years following the Roman conquest, as the later settlement was not comparable with the earlier one on the site. Continuity from the pre-conquest period is attested at such other sites as Norsey Wood at Billericay, Essex, and Park Brow, Sussex. The latter is of particular interest in its possession of village remains dated to the bronze and iron ages as well as to the Roman period, demonstrating considerable longevity of settlement on that site. The site below the Thundersbarrow hillfort may represent the forced removal of the local population out of their defended iron age enclosure into an open village which would have provided no potential threat to the Roman authorities (figure 23). Other small sites maintained much of their iron age culture and were affected by the Roman conquest to only a slight degree, as was suggested for the sites of Tallington in Lincolnshire and Maxey in Cambridgeshire, which were compared by their excavator to sites such as Huckhoe on the northern frontier, as their economy was of the iron age type.

Although agriculture was primary to the economy of these villages, some sites yielded evidence for industrial activity, sometimes on quite a large scale. In the Norfolk Fens, for example, the settlement at Denver revealed evidence for extensive salt working, which was also found at Chalton in Hampshire. The latter site was also involved in the manufacture of pottery. At Maxey, Cambridgeshire, evidence was found for both iron and bronze working and metalworking has been suggested at a number of other sites. The small settlement of Little Down, on Lansdown near Bath (figure 9), was heavily engaged in the large-scale industrial production of both iron and, more significantly, pewter tablewares, presumably aimed at the nearby prosperous market of Bath. The profits from such industrial activity as well as those from the sale of any farming surpluses or products such as wool, leather and dairy produce would have enabled the villagers to purchase luxury items like fine pottery and metalwork, which were presumably made available by itinerant traders or tinkers who plied their trade between these often isolated settlements, off the main roadways.

23. The Thundersbarrow hillfort, with its associated Romano-British settlement and fields. (After Cunliffe.)

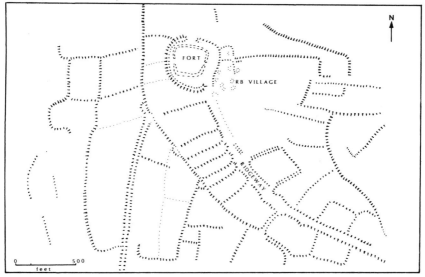

24. The settlement at Chisenbury Warren, Wiltshire. (Photograph: University of Cambridge copyright reserved.)
25. The distribution of Romano-British sites on the Lansdown plateau, near Bath.

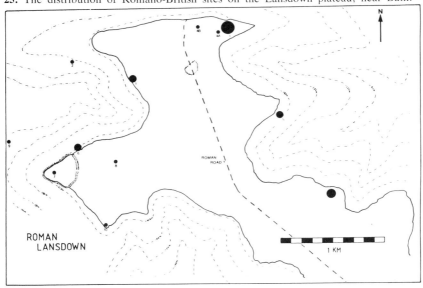

ROMAN
LANSDOWN

ROMAN
ROAD ?

1 KM

N

5
Prosperous large villages

The villages examined in the previous chapter exhibited a number of Romanised features but they owed much more to their iron age origins than to the new Roman regime and may therefore be viewed as 'native' rather than 'Roman'. The settlements considered in this chapter were often of considerable size, extending over many acres. They demonstrate a far greater degree of Romanisation than any of the sites already examined and in archaeological terms they illustrate the economic and social benefits which the marketing exploitation of the province could bring. The villages of this type were closely linked to the economy of the province and the majority were therefore to be found located along either side of the major Roman roads, as at Catsgore in Somerset (figure 26). The excavation and survey of this settlement revealed the remains of both buildings and enclosures over a large area on both sides of the Roman road, on which the village was based.

The prosperous and highly Romanised nature of these large communities is normally very apparent during excavation. As with the small villages, the presence of coins on these sites testifies to a monetary economy, but to a far greater degree. Fine pottery wares are also frequently found, with samian being replaced in the third and fourth centuries by British finewares. The standard rectangular form of building, with many variations, is to be found on all these sites and examples of the different forms which such buildings could take are seen at Catsgore (figure 26) where there are simple rectangular buildings as well as instances of both aisled and apsidal-ended types. Some of these houses could be very grand as in the villa-type building at Catsgore and the finely furnished and equipped examples from the Cambridgeshire Fens, which bear a close resemblance to Roman town houses.

The publication by T. W. Potter of the evidence from a concentrated programme of aerial survey, field walking and excavation carried out in the central Fens has provided a number of good examples of these prosperous and highly Romanised settlements within a comparatively small area (see Further reading). Because these developments occurred in a landscape which had been largely cleared of pre-Roman occupation by extensive flooding, the Roman settlements owed very little to

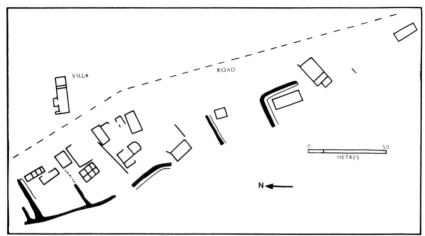

26. The village site at Catsgore, Somerset, as it was in the fourth century AD. Note the large villa-type building to the east and the location of the other buildings within ditched, banked and sometimes walled enclosures. (After Leech.)

any iron age predecessors and were thus perhaps more amenable to Roman influences. There also appears to have been a considerable level of imperial influence in this reclaimed region during the later first and second centuries AD and it was probably as a result of this imperial involvement that the villages emerged. Indeed, the lack of villas within the area of the Cambridgeshire Fens has frequently led to the suggestion that the area was an imperial estate on which villa settlement was forbidden. In effect it would have been the emperor's personal land and the villagers within it would have been his tenants. This suggestion has been strengthened by the excavation of a large Hadrianic tower at Stonea Grange (figure 27), which may well represent the administrative centre of the imperial estate in the early second century. Direct imperial involvement can also be seen in the substantial dyke system constructed in the area in this period.

Four large villages of between 25 and 40 acres (about 10-15 ha) have been located in this programme of study, situated on 'islands' in the peat fen, and these are suggested as being centres of the Roman occupation of the area. The sites are those at Stonea, Grandford, Flaggrass and Coldham (figure 28); Flaggrass and Grandford are situated on the Roman-built Fen Causeway which traversed the Fens in this period. These large villages formed the focus for various complexes of small enclosures, all linked by droveways. In addition to these settlements there were a number of smaller occupation centres, such as the small site at Waldersea, as well as a number of simple farmsteads, such as that excavated at the Golden Lion site. The vast majority of these centres appeared in the second century, probably as a result of Hadrianic and Antonine impetus to settlement in the region, although a few of the larger villages, as at Stonea and Grandford, revealed evidence for pre-Flavian (mid first-century AD) occupation. At Grandford (figure 29) there appears to have been a mid first-century fort which may have acted as a focus for the development of a fortside *vicus* of the type already seen on the northern frontier. Stonea, as well as providing evidence for iron age occupation, produced the earliest Roman levels, with remains dated to the period AD 50-70. The subsequent impetus to settlement in the second century is demonstrated by the rapid development of the village of Coldham and, although much of the Fens was flooded in the earlier third century, in the later third and fourth centuries the larger sites in the area flourished greatly.

27. Stonea in the Cambridgeshire Fens: the main excavated area looking south down a street, with side streets coming in from the left. (Photograph: T. Potter).

Good evidence for the early prosperity of these villages comes from Grandford, where substantial timber-framed buildings on low platforms were erected about AD 90.

The occupants were sufficiently affluent to use clay tiles on their roofs and the plots on this site were individually laid out in an organised fashion, akin to that visible at the site of Catsgore in Somerset (figure 26). After the third century there was extensive rebuilding at Grandford, with the use of imported stone from the east Midlands to construct large stone houses with tiled roofs, plastered and whitewashed walls and glazed windows, demonstrating the prosperity of the community during the later Roman period. Such was also the case at Stonea, where there was a wealthy sanctuary dedicated to the Roman goddess Minerva, her worship being attested in the finds of a votive plaque and a bronze bust, both of high-quality workmanship. A large semi-industrial site has also been located close to the Fen Causeway at

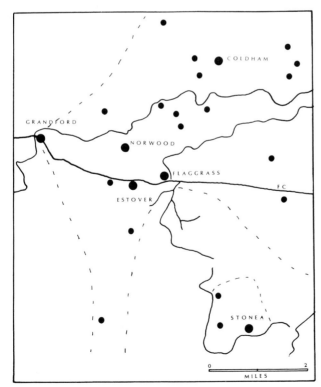

28. The distribution of large village sites in the Cambridgeshire Fens. 'FC' marks the Roman Fen Causeway. (After Potter.)

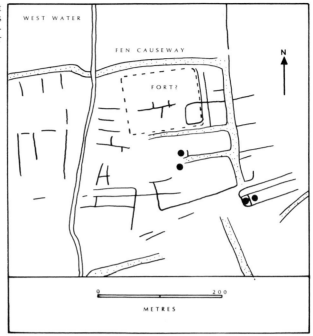

29. The Fen site at Grandford. The dots mark suggested building plots. (After Potter).

WEST WATER

FEN CAUSEWAY

FORT?

N

0   200

METRES

Norwood, positioned beside a tidal river. Here there was evidence for the organised and extensive production of salt, visible in the finds of briquetage and other saltmaking debris over many acres and in the discovery of two clay-built tanks, which were probably used to collect salt by evaporating sea water. It seems certain that the large-scale production of salt was a major part of the Fenland economy.

The excavations in the region appear to disprove the traditional view that the Fens were one of the principal arable centres of the province. The area should, according to the excavator of these sites, rather be seen as being more important for its pastoral economy, with a number of sites yielding valuable evidence for such pastoralism. Animal bone studies show that sheep were of the greatest importance in the region, with the age of the bones indicating that the animals were kept for their wool rather than for their meat. Frequent finds of spindle whorls strengthen the view that the Fens were probably an important wool-producing region. The larger villages were no doubt centres for the production of woollen cloth and the good position of sites such as

Flaggrass on routes of communication would have been significant. In terms of such a sheep-based economy the Fens might usefully be compared to the Gloucestershire Cotswolds in both the Roman and the medieval periods. Cattle were also of importance within the Fens and a complex trade has been suggested in such commodities as meat, leather and hides, as well as in salt and woollen cloth. It was no doubt this organised trade which formed the basis for the wealth of such sites as Grandford and the sites exhibit the rewards of the successful economic exploitation of the resources of their area.

Catsgore

The excavations at Catsgore, in Somerset, constitute one of the most important pieces of work yet undertaken on a lowland Roman village site and it therefore merits special consideration. The site (figure 26) is another good example of a large and fairly prosperous village, comparable to the Fenland sites. The first major developments on the site occurred in the second century AD, with the construction of a number of curious polygonal buildings, which appear to have been timber-framed on narrow sill walls. Each lay in a separate embanked enclosure, suggested by the excavator as indicating individual farming complexes (figure 26). During the second, third and fourth centuries these units were rapidly developed, with the replacement of the polygonal buildings by stone-built structures of various forms. Some were interpreted as being for domestic use, whilst others probably had an agricultural function. The apsidal-ended buildings are one of the more curious features of the site. In the fourth century the earth boundaries were removed and replaced in stone, illustrating their continued observance. The organised settlement to the west of the Roman road appears to contrast with that to the east, revealed primarily by geophysical survey, where there were no separate enclosures and the occupation pattern appears to have been of a much more organic nature.

6
Small towns

A number of the larger villages in Roman Britain have been grouped together under the vague title of 'small towns'. As there are no criteria applied to the use of the term (unlike villas, for example), a vast cross-section of sites has been rather unsatisfactorily grouped together.

The use of this description is therefore fraught with difficulties, but until a replacement term is found students of Roman Britain must suffer with it. As will be seen in chapter 8, the Latin term of *vicus* might be applied rather more agreeably to many of the settlements which fall into the small town grouping, but the meaning of even this title is subject to much academic controversy and therefore, in this chapter, the term 'small town' will continue to be used.

The settlements that fall within this grouping are basically large roadside sites, providing services to the Roman road users and utilising the road system to distribute their industrial and agricultural products. Not all of the sites are positioned on such major Roman roads as the Fosse Way and Watling Street. Many were on less important routes which are no longer traceable, as may have been the case at the large sites of Wycomb and Kingscote in the Gloucestershire Cotswolds (figures 30 and 31) and at Kelvedon in Essex. It has been suggested that the iron age site at Kelvedon on which the small town is based may have been of greater importance in deciding the site location than any major Roman road. It is also likely that iron age Kelvedon would have been served by a road anyway.

All the small towns were of considerable size (hence the term) but, even so, there was much diversity in site extents. At Godmanchester, Cambridgeshire, the walled later Roman settlement occupied some 20 acres (8 ha), a little less than the walled sites of Irchester in Northamptonshire, and Cambridge. In contrast, the fortified settlement at Ancaster, Lincolnshire, was of only 10 acres (4 ha) but, as at a number of other walled sites, there was evidence for substantial occupation beyond the fortified circuit. A similar size diversity existed in the case of the undefended sites. Kelvedon occupied between 15 and 20 acres (6-8 ha) whilst Kingscote was of over 80 acres (32 ha), with Oundle, Northamptonshire, covering a similar size.

Despite their large size, the majority of these sites are

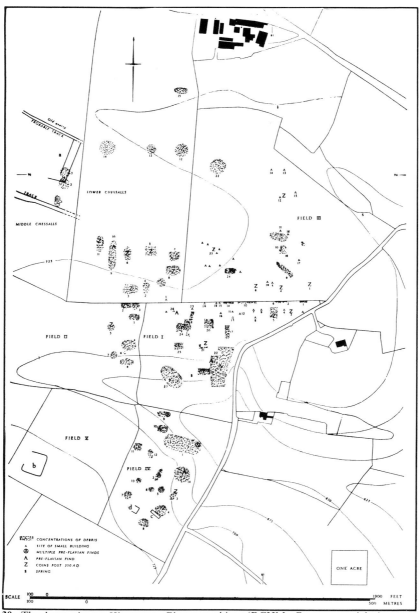

30. The large site at Kingscote, Gloucestershire. (RCHM: Crown copyright.)

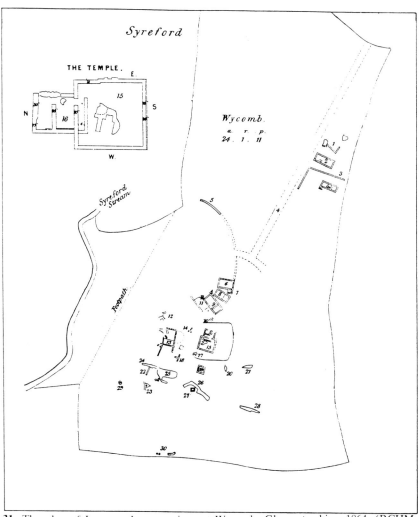

31. The plan of Lawrence's excavations at Wycomb, Gloucestershire, 1864. (RCHM: Crown copyright.)

considerably smaller than the true towns of Roman Britain — the *coloniae* and the tribal capitals. The buildings within the small towns also tended to be more spread out than within the compact municipal street grids *(insulae)*. Therefore, despite their size and the fact that some were fortified, it is still possible to view the small towns as village-type settlements and this view is strengthened by their essentially rural rather than urban nature. In this ruralism, as well as in their siting and development patterns, they closely resemble the many medieval villages which grew up alongside important routes of communication. Both types of settlement share a similar roadside ribbon development pattern, as can be seen at such Roman sites as Chelmsford (figure 32) and Springhead in Kent (figure 34).

A number of other features differentiates these sites from the true towns, most being things which should be expected as standard in any Roman urban centre. These include a well laid-out street grid forming *insulae,* and the normal range of public buildings — the *forum, basilica* and baths. All of these amenities were basic necessities for all Roman towns, but they are significantly absent in the case of the small towns. Some sites possess one or two of these features, as at Godmanchester, where the excavator suggested the existence of baths and a basilica, but no small town site possesses all of them. In the Roman sense these settlement types would be viewed as rural rather than urban and the evidence presented below should demonstrate that they may not be termed urban in any other sense either.

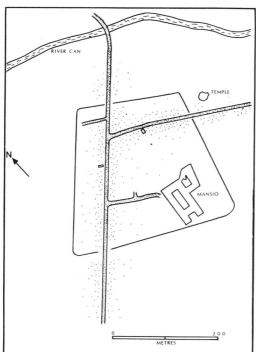

32. *Caesaromagnus,* the small town at Chelmsford, Essex. Dots indicate roadside settlement. (Chelmsford Archaeological Trust.)

33. The small town at Kenchester, near Hereford. Note the side streets and building outlines. (Photograph: University of Cambridge copyright reserved.)

A vital factor in assigning the term 'village' to the majority of these sites is their essentially agricultural nature, despite their size and common prosperity, with agriculture forming the economic mainstay of the settlement. The large site at Godmanchester, Cambridgeshire, presents a good example of this element in the prosperity of the settlement. Behind the main street frontages the excavators found a number of farming complexes associated with a range of small agricultural structures, such as drying racks for corn and pit granaries, some of which still contained their Roman grain. Survey work in the region of the site has revealed much of the large field system which surrounded and supported the settlement. The roadside village of Camerton in Avon (figure 35) in the third and fourth centuries AD supported a thriving pewter industry which supplied its products to customers throughout the West Country. Nevertheless, there was still much evidence for agricultural activity in the form of tools for cultivation as well as in finds associated with the secondary activities of corn milling (quern stones) and the spinning and weaving of wool (spindle whorls).

It has been suggested that the small towns were largely self-supporting in terms of primary products such as grain, meat and dairy produce as well as in the production of basic necessities like cloth, tools and some of the coarser pottery wares found on these sites. The opposite is the case with the true urban centres, which are viewed as being 'parasitic' on the countryside, unable to produce all the food and other essentials that were required by the artisans and administrators who inhabited them. In this respect town and small town were fundamentally different. The former was wholly urban and productively specialised in the provision of fine manufactured goods, services (baths, temples, markets and so on) and administration, whereas the small towns were essentially rural, villages whose large size was primarily due to the economic stimulus provided by the Roman road system. The small towns appear to have been a response to the marketing potential offered by the Roman roads as well as by the development of the potentially valuable markets of town and villa. To that extent they were artificial creations and therefore wholly Roman institutions.

Origins

A number of these sites demonstrate evidence for iron age origins: for example, in Oxfordshire the sites of Lower Lea and Woodeaton produced much iron age material. Lower Lea was sited near a prehistoric hillfort, whence presumably came the population of the Roman settlement. A large iron age presence is also suggested for the site of Ancaster, Lincolnshire, although the comparable walled site at *Margidunum,* Nottinghamshire (figure 36), possessed no such evidence. In the territory of the Trinovantes, in Essex and south and east Suffolk, a number of small towns demonstrate evidence for iron age roots, with the possible failed tribal capital of Chelmsford being the only major exception. Kelvedon was a major iron age centre, as was Braughing, Hertfordshire, which was prosperous enough to mint its own coins. The port site of Heybridge also attests to such continuity and the large numbers of *amphorae* (the standard Roman storage vessel for liquids) show that the site was trading with Roman merchants in the pre-conquest period. In some instances there is evidence for iron age activity, but on a scale which was not comparable with the later Roman settlement. Such was the case at Camerton, Avon (figure 35), where an iron age roundhouse was excavated.

Many small towns appear to have originated as fortside villages *(vici),* comparable to the examples already seen on the northern frontier. As in the north, such *vici* tended to grow up near the fort gates, because the forts were often the most valuable focus of trade in an area in the first century, as a result of the unique spending power of the resident troops, whose pay formed the basis for the province's monetary economy. The *vici* therefore

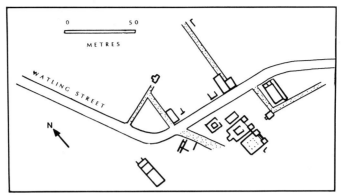

34. Springhead, Kent. Note the large roadside temple complex. (After Detsicas.)

attracted merchants and artisans, as well as the unofficial families of the soldiers, forced to live outside the fort walls. Retired veterans from the fort's garrison also sometimes stayed within these settlements, thereby increasing their wealth. At Godmanchester the ditches and rampart of one of the series of forts in the strategic Great Ouse valley have been uncovered and at Chelmsford (figure 32) finds included military equipment, Claudian pottery of the mid first century AD and early timber buildings of military type, all probably from a conquest-period fort on that site. Other small towns with proven fort origins include *Margidunum* (Nottinghamshire, figure 36), Sea Mills (Avon), Mildenhall (Wiltshire) and Alchester (Oxfordshire). Some small towns, however, demonstrated no military origins, including Springhead (Kent, figure 34), Dunstable (Bedfordshire) and Bourton-on-the-Water in the Cotswolds.

Site development

The large settlement at Bourton-on-the-Water in the Gloucestershire Cotswolds provides a very good example of the economic forces which served to promote the development of the small towns, for although many sites originated as fortside villages it was economic factors alone which caused them to develop and flourish. At Bourton the centre of iron age occupation was Salmonsbury hillfort, located on the prehistoric Jurassic Way, the ancient track which ran along the Cotswold ridge. Following the construction of the Fosse Way some thousand yards (900 metres) to the west of the hillfort and the creation of a crossing point over the river Windrush, there was a population shift towards the new road, which now replaced the Jurassic Way as the most important economic artery in the region. It was apparent that the people from Salmonsbury populated the new settlement because of the continued use of some pottery forms and also because the Roman period site stretched back into the hillfort, which was linked to the Fosse by a metalled trackway. The new small town of Bourton covered some 30 acres (12 ha) and was situated on either side of the Fosse Way in a ribbon development on both sides of the river crossing, which was located during excavations. The settlement area spread up nearby Whiteshoots Hill as well as back into the hillfort.

The linear roadside development of this site, so commonly seen in medieval villages, is typical of many small sites. This is also the case with the excavated buildings. These were interpreted as an apsidal-ended 'wayside shrine', an industrial building associated with a forge and ovens, a bakehouse, a row of open-fronted shops and a possible posting house or inn *(mansio)*. These buildings were designed to provide the road user with all the services that he might require, probably including a bed for the night in the *mansio*. The location of the settlement 15 miles (24 km) from the town of Cirencester, to the south-west, would probably have made Bourton a popular stopping place for travellers through the Cotswolds. Their custom appears to have brought great wealth to the site, revealed in the discovery of rich house remains, including mosaic pavements and hypocaust heating systems.

A similar ribbon development is apparent at the site of Springhead, Kent (figure 34), and at Godmanchester, Cambridgeshire, where the crossing of the river Ouse formed the focus for the development of the settlement. As stated previously, Bourton-on-the-Water in Gloucestershire possessed a number of streets leading off the Fosse Way and rudimentary street plans have been noted at a number of other sites, where some degree of internal organisation and planning is suggested. Such plans are not comparable with the regular gridded *insulae* system of urban centres like Silchester, but basic settlement organisation is suggested at such sites as Godmanchester, Chelmsford (figure 32), Camerton (Avon, figure 35), Springhead (Kent, figure 34) and Dorn (Gloucestershire), as well as at the centres at Alchester (Oxfordshire) and Catterick (North Yorkshire). The plan of Camerton (figure 35) shows that some of the buildings were located facing the Fosse Way, which ran through the settlement, whilst others were at right angles to it and aligned alongside the metalled streets which led off the Fosse, with the suggestion of a basic grid. Alchester, Oxfordshire, also has the suggestion of a grid visible in its site plan and similar building alignment is known

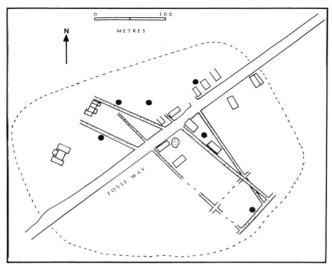

35. Camerton, Avon. The dots represent building sites. Note the two winged-corridor villa-type buildings. (After Wedlake.)

from Chelmsford and Great Chesterford, Essex.

The provision of services for travellers seen at Bourton is also apparent at a number of other small town sites. The most significant buildings relating to such services are the *mansiones*. These were the posting stations of the Roman roads, providing overnight accommodation as well as food and stabling in a manner comparable to the later medieval inns. Large *mansiones* have been excavated at Godmanchester and Chelmsford (figure 32). The former had an associated baths complex and the latter dominated the walled area of the site. Some villages are likely to have been legally bound to provide services for users of the main roads (the *cursus publicus*), as was the case in other provinces.

Another service to the road user was the provision of roadside temples, as seen at the important site at Springhead, Kent (figure 34), where there was a large religious complex alongside Watling Street between Canterbury and London. Here a large walled temple area was constructed in the second century, provided with an entrance building and decorated with fine mosaic floors and painted plaster walls. The siting of this temple complex may well have been due to the springs on the site, thereby relating Springhead to the other great spring-based temple site at Bath. A large temple was also excavated at Wycomb in Gloucestershire (figure 31), possibly associated with a large amphitheatre of a type similar to that suggested at Bath.

The great spa and temple complex of Bath cannot be viewed as a village, as it is a unique site. However, it is of great interest in its possession of fine third- and fourth-century town houses, comparable to those suggested already at Bourton-on-the-Water. At Camerton, Avon (figure 35), there are two 'classic' winged-corridor villa-type buildings located within the settlement and contemporary with it. Their excavation revealed mosaic pavements, painted wall plaster and well-sculpted architectural fragments. Other fine town or villa-type corridor buildings have been excavated at Great Chesterford, Essex, and at *Margidunum,* Nottinghamshire (figure 36). Because these buildings so closely resemble traditional villa forms some archaeologists have suggested that they represent the dwelling of traditional 'villa owners', who founded and owned the associated rural settlement. There are certainly examples of large villages being found in direct association with a probable villa estate in the traditional sense, for example at Rivenhall, Essex, and also possibly at Westland, Somerset. Such might also be the case at Kingscote in Gloucestershire (figure 30), where a very large villa-like building complex lies beside an extensive small town. Villa-type buildings are being increasingly found within the true Roman towns, such as at Cirencester, making it likely that the 'villas' at such sites as Camerton and *Margidunum* merely represent the presence within the settlement of people of sufficient affluence to build large luxurious houses of this type. They should not, therefore, be linked to the normal view of the villa and the villa estate.

An alternative view is that some of these buildings may have been built to house Roman officials connected with the administration of the local area. Inscriptions tell of the presence of military policemen *(centuriones regionarii)* at Bath and Dorchester and other such offices may have been involved in the collection of the local tax *(annona)* from the landholders in the area. Connected with this idea is the suggestion that some of the small towns may have acted as the administrative centres for their local tribal areas *(pagi)*. The role of these settlements in connection with the *pagi* will be examined in chapter 8.

Another aspect of these sites linked with imperial activity on a provincial level is their role in the defence of Britain from both internal and external forces. A number of these villages were walled at varying stages in their development, as were villages all over the empire. The first such defences were the simple earthwork circuits erected around a few sites at the end of the second century, possibly as a result of the rebellion of Albinus. Such examples are *Margidunum,* Nottinghamshire (figure 36),

and Chelmsford (figure 32). A number of small towns subse-
quently received stone defences, as at Godmanchester, Cambridgeshire, as part of a general programme of fortification
visible in the majority of towns in Britain, which received their
main defences at this time. Work continued into the fourth
century, as at Mildenhall, Wiltshire, and a number of pre-existing
circuits were strengthened still further with the addition of
external towers, as at Ancaster, Lincolnshire. This work of the
fourth century is likely to be associated with the general policy of
consolidation carried out by Count Theodosius.

The fortification of small towns was far from a uniform policy,
however, and a number of large sites remained undefended, like
the 80 acre (32 ha) site at Kingscote, Gloucestershire (figure 30)
and those at Braughing in Hertfordshire, Springhead and
Maidstone in Kent and Lower Lea, Oxfordshire. It seems likely,
therefore, that villages were walled not so much because of

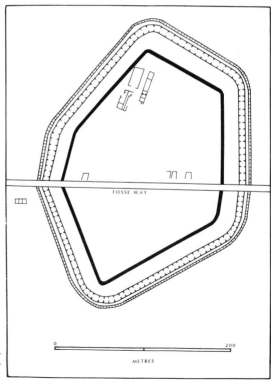

36. *Margidunum*, the defended small town in Nottinghamshire. (After Todd).

imperial concern for the safety of the villagers, but rather as part of a national scheme for the defence of the province as a whole and the strategic positions of many small towns should be remembered in this context. As many sites originated as fortside settlements, and most forts were strategically located, the small towns inherited these strategic positions. These positions might be at a crossroads or river crossing for example. When the military left the site, as they had done in most cases by the end of the first century, the village could use its strategic position to economic advantage. It may therefore have been thought necessary in the third century to create a series of fortified posts, scattered throughout the countryside on the major routes of communication, as on the Fosse Way at such sites as Dorn (Gloucestershire), Ancaster (Lincolnshire) and *Margidunum* (Nottinghamshire, figure 36). Many sites close to the Fosse Way were left undefended, however, as at Camerton, Avon (figure 35) and Kingscote, Gloucestershire (figure 30). There were also a number of defended small town sites on Stane Street, the London to Chichester road, such as at Hardham, West Sussex. That route also yielded evidence for large sites remaining undefended, for example the site of about 70 acres (24 ha) at Ewell. Similarly, on the road between Canterbury and London Rochester was defended but Springhead was not.

A complicating factor has been noted at a number of these fortified sites, as at *Margidunum* (figure 36), where it is apparent that there were large open spaces within the walled enclosure and extensive settlement outside it. A similar situation existed at the 26 acre (10.5 ha) walled site at Alchester, Oxfordshire. This has led to the suggestion that some of these enclosures may not have been primarily intended for civilian use, but principally for the mobile field armies of the later Roman period, as regional bases. Some might have also been fortified police posts *(burgus),* as was suggested for Gatcombe, near Bristol, although this was probably the site of a large defended villa complex. The site of Chelmsford, with its prominent *mansio* (figure 32), may indicate that some of these enclosures were designed to provide fortified posting house stations.

Economic activity

These settlements played an important role within the province as vital centres of both production and distribution. The evidence for large-scale agriculture has already been examined, but a number of small towns attest to highly organised and widely distributed industrial production. Many sites also appear to have been of considerable importance as local market centres, and many appear to have produced pottery on a large scale, as was the case at Mildenhall, Wiltshire, and Mancetter, Warwickshire. The Nene Valley finewares were produced at Chesterton, and Water Newton was the centre for the Castor industries. The large site at Congresbury in Avon was the base for the distinctive local greyware industry and many kilns were found during excavations over a wide area.

Evidence for metallurgy is also commonplace, as at Braughing, Hertfordshire, where bronze and iron goods were produced in the third century. Similar evidence for metalworking comes from a number of Trinovantian sites and at Kelvedon in Essex there was also evidence for tile manufacturing. At Springhead, Kent, both tile manufacturing and a considerable amount of ironworking were carried out in the third century.

During the third and fourth centuries the pewter industry flourished, with its distinctive range of tablewares. Pewter

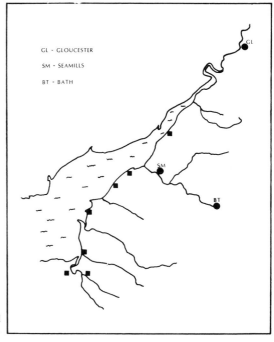

37. The distribution of coastal settlements down the Severn.

production was especially prevalent in the West Country and evidence for it, in the form of moulds and slag, has been found extensively at Camerton in Avon (figure 35), as well as at Nettleton, Wiltshire, where pewter manufacturing replaced the temple of Apollo found there as the mainstay of the economy of the settlements. Both sites possessed the standard rectangular stone workshops, the products from which were widely distributed, being found especially on villa sites in the region. Such a find was made during the dramatic villa excavations at Brislington in Bristol, where a whole pewter dinner service was recovered from a well, along with the remains of its probable owners, who had presumably been the victims of a raid up the river Avon by Irish pirates. Connected to this was a lead-mining site at Charterhouse-on-Mendip. This settlement was founded under imperial control within a few years of the Roman conquest, to facilitate the mining and exporting of the valuable Mendip lead reserves. The site is a good example of a small town involved in primary production.

Some of these small towns appear to have functioned as ports, as did Heybridge in Trinovantian territory, and inland ports have been suggested as such sites as Ilchester and Chelmsford, where there were possible wharves on the riverside (figure 32). An examination of the likely small town sites on the east coast of the Severn estuary demonstrates the presence of possible ports at regular intervals (figure 37). At Sea Mills and Bawdrip there is evidence for the presence of warehouses on the dockside, as well as for a considerable level of trade in commodities transported in Spanish-made *amphorae,* such as olive oil, wine and fish sauce *(garum).* This trade may well have been mainly with Gaul and Spain, although there is evidence for a livestock trade existing between Somerset and South Wales in the medieval period.

Villas often cluster around these small towns rather than around the major urban centres and this is the case at Kingscote, Chesterton, Ancaster and *Margidunum,* as well as at many other sites, and the small towns appear to have performed a vital role as both market centres and market places, as suggested as Godmanchester and Chesterton, near Peterborough. At Chesterton the presence of a large meat market is attested by the finds of great numbers of butchered animal bones. Shops have been found at a variety of sites, like Braughing, Hertfordshire, and Bourton-on-the-Water, Gloucestershire. These large rural centres probably performed a similar distributary function to that of the medieval villages, holding weekly markets for the sale of such things as perishable foodstuffs and also by holding seasonal fairs, at which corn, livestock and manufactured goods could be bought and sold. The farm or villa owner would probably have visited his local small town market or fair in order to sell his surplus arable produce and the wool or cloth from his sheep and to buy cattle, or manufactured goods like fine pottery or iron tools, which might be produced either in the settlement itself or be made available by itinerant merchants, who probably also acted as middlemen in the channelling of these primary products into the nearest urban centre. There is probably good evidence from all of the small town sites for the extensive use of a monetary economy. Whilst in the small town, visitors might have stopped to worship in the local shrine or to pay their annual taxes to a resident or visiting official.

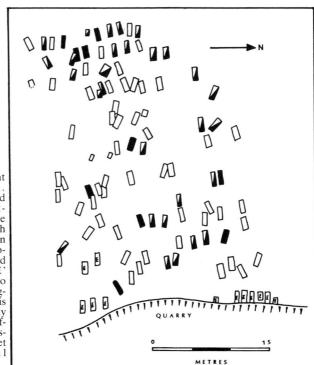

38. The cemetery at Camerton, Avon. Suggested Roman and immediately post-Roman graves are blocked in, those with probable pagan Saxon grave goods are diagonally blocked, and those marked 'E' point east and have no grave goods. The suggested date range is late Roman to early Christian Saxon. (After Horne, by permission of the Somerset Archaeological Society.)

7
Villages in sub-Roman Britain

There is little to indicate any great decline in the fortunes of village-type settlements during the fourth century in Britain; indeed, in the early part of the century there is a considerable body of evidence which attests to a high level of prosperity and activity. This prosperity is seen in the large villages in the central Fens, as well as at such industrially based sites as Camerton (figure 35) and Little Down (figure 9), both in Avon. These settlements appear to have experienced the economic boom current throughout the province in the earlier fourth century at least, visible both in the towns and in the villas. The villas enjoyed their greatest prosperity in this period, as seen in the large villa complexes of south-east and south-west England. Differential prosperity did, however, become apparent as the fourth century wore on. This diversity is best illustrated by the towns: some like Cirencester prospered, whereas Leicester and Wroxeter began a sharp decline. This contrast is also visible in the villages: in Sussex and Hampshire, for example, there is a confused situation, with sites like Park Brow being abandoned, while others, such as Chalton, show a marked development. This has led to the suggestion that in the late fourth century the rural population became concentrated in village-type settlements. This did not occur at the large walled site of Godmanchester, Cambridgeshire, where there was decline and abandonment at this time. As was described in chapter 3, the highland areas of Britain were affected to only a slight degree by the Roman conquest and the situation was probably little different at the ending of Roman administration. At Huckhoe in Northumberland, for example, village life appears to have continued unaltered into the early medieval period.

A problem which soon becomes apparent to any archaeologist attempting to assess the evidence for continuity of settlement in both highlands and lowlands is the difficulty in demonstrating continuous occupation, on lowland sites especially, because of the presence of later settlements, either medieval or modern, on the same site. Where evidence for Roman occupation is found, it does not necessarily mean that the settlement has been continuously inhabited. If, for example, the Roman village was sited in a prime situation on a river crossing or valley floor, it is likely that subsequent settlers would have chosen to inhabit the same position. This applies particularly to the many lowland areas which were extensively resettled in the early medieval period. An example of this problem can be seen at the site of the deserted medieval village at Upton, Gloucestershire, where excavations revealed Roman remains. So did the settlement continue, or had the Roman site been long deserted when the medieval village was founded? The occurrence of Saxon pottery on that site might possibly weight the arguments towards continuity.

A number of lowland sites do, however, demonstrate evidence for continuity, or it can be strongly suspected. There is proof of early Germanic settlers being present at the Essex sites of Heybridge and Rivenhall and at Chelmsford it is suggested that the lack of evidence for German settlement in the fifth and sixth centuries might indicate the continued occupation of the small town by its original Romano-British population.

Outside the areas of early Germanic migrations, in south-west England, there is good evidence for continuity, as at Camerton (figure 35). Near to the industrial settlement there is a cemetery which appears to span the period from the late fourth century, through the pagan Saxon period and into the Christian early medieval period. This is visible in the varied groupings of graves of different alignments, associated with different grave goods (figure 38).

In Somerset there appears to have been a widespread transference of village settlements back into the local iron age hillforts, presumably as a result of instability in the countryside. At Cannington the Roman population appears to have shifted from the vulnerable port site of Combwich up into the iron age hillfort, outside which there is a very large sub-Roman cemetery, which may have been used until the medieval period, when the present village of Cannington was founded.

The study of place-names can also be very informative in any attempts to trace continuity of Roman sites. The place-name 'wicham' is a good example, as it seems to represent Anglo-Saxon recognition of a continuing Romano-British settlement and is probably derived from a corruption of the Latin term *vicus*. The site of Wycomb, Gloucestershire, is a likely example and Braughing, Hertfordshire, has an associated 'wicham' field name. Similar significance can also be attached to the name 'chessells', known from such large sites as Bourton-on-the-Water and Kingscote in Gloucestershire.

8
Villages in other provinces

An examination of the evidence from other provinces in the form of inscriptions and other historical data, especially that which relates to the status and role of villages, is of great value in the study of similar settlements in Roman Britain. Such a comparison is necessary because virtually no evidence of this sort is to be found in Britain. However, what applies in one province does not necessarily do so in another. This evidence merely enables us to suggest what might have been the case and therefore allows the bare archaeological record to be supplemented with historical data.

The province which can be most closely compared to Britain is Gaul, which shared many similarities, although it was Romanised to a far greater degree because of its longer period of Roman occupation. In Gaul, the *pagi* have been defined as being the internal tribal groupings, perhaps akin territorially to modern parishes. It has been suggested that at the centre of each *pagus* was a *vicus,* the Latin term meaning a settlement like a village and used by French archaeologists to describe the small town-like settlements which they excavated.

All of the Gallic inscriptions relating to *vici* have been found on major Roman roads. Other similarities between the Gallic *vici* and the British small towns can be seen in such things as settlement origins. The site at Arlon may usefully be compared with that at Bourton-on-the-Water, Gloucestershire, as at both sites the iron age population moved from the old iron age centre down to the new Roman road. At Velzebe a fort preceded the later small town, a familiar occurrence.

The Gallic *vici* are also envisaged as being important production and distribution centres, with villas lying close by, as in Britain. Many of the sites demonstrate evidence for considerable agricultural activity, as at Arlon. Finally, many of the Gallic *vici* were fortified in the later Roman period and the area enclosed was often very small. At the site of Birtby there was evidence for extensive occupation, both inside and outside the walled area. A number of these defended villages appear to have acted as fortified strongpoints, stationed along the arterial roads.

Gaul provides evidence for a well ordered local administrative structure with reference being made to village magistrates and to the institution of the village council *(ordo)* within the larger

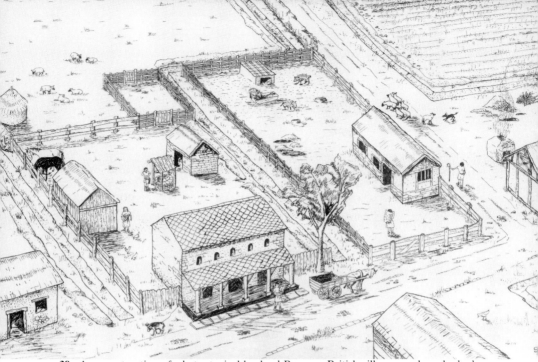

39. A reconstruction of what a typical lowland Romano-British village may have looked like, with different types of building located in individual plots along the roadside, with a strong agricultural element. (Drawing by Sarah Lucy.)

settlements. It was probably these rich members of the rural administration who owned and lived in the fine houses found at such sites as Naix, which are comparable to the villa-type buildings found in a number of British small towns and mentioned in chapter 6. An inscription from the village of Le Heraple testifies to the presence of another type of person within the settlement, the local merchant *(negotiator)*.

An important difference between the *vici* of Gaul and the small towns of Britain is their size: some of the Gallic sites were very large and were of quasi-urban status and appearance (Arlon, for example, covered some 60 acres, 25 ha), although in Britain such sites as Godmanchester are likely to have had some form of urban status. Nevertheless, it seems likely from the evidence in Gaul that a number of the small towns of Britain would have been termed *vici* in the Roman period, although the use of that word can be fraught with as many difficulties as are associated with the term 'small towns', for the definition of *vicus* is the subject of academic controversy. It does seem likely, however, that by the fourth century at least the term had degenerated into meaning a village of any type.

Information from other provinces can be equally enlightening as that from Gaul. In the eastern province, for example, the urban centres appear to have had vast territories which encompassed a number of villages, the inhabitants of which paid taxes and rents to the towns. Such is the case in Roman Thrace. It is possible that in Britain a similar situation may have applied on a smaller scale. The town of Gloucester has a number of villages in very close proximity and they may have been within the *territorium* of that town. Some other villages appear to have been owned by individuals, such as the *Vicus Quintionis* in Thrace and the *Vicus Annaei* in Africa, both named after their owner or patron, and it has already been suggested that this might have applied to the sites of Rivenhall, Kingscote and Westland in Britain. Other settlements were owned by affluent temple complexes, as in the example of the Syrian temple to Doliche at Baitocaece. Small towns like Springhead might be British examples of such temple ownership.

Further evidence for village administration comes from the province of Moesia, where there are inscriptions relating to the existence of the magistrates and *ordo* attested in Gaul, as well as for another village officer, the *quinquennalis*. The Theodosian code of the fourth century refers to villages as administrative centres and also to the existence of 'mother villages', which are probably administrative units founded to act as the political centre for a number of villages.

The important marketing role of the villages is attested in a large number of provinces and the market villages in Africa were given the official title of *nundinae*. The holding of large seasonal fairs is also known, as at Skaptopara in Thrace, whose inhabitants complained to the emperor about the large fair which was held close to their village. All the evidence suggests that the larger villages of the empire fulfilled a vital function as market centres.

To what extent information of this sort can be applied to Roman Britain will never be known, but villages formed one of the most vital economic and administrative units of the empire and it is likely that the majority of the empire's population lived in these types of communities. It is therefore through the examination of these types of settlements that we are best able to assess the impact of Roman government upon the native population of the provinces, for the inhabitants of these settlements were essentially native in origin.

9
Museums to visit

The following museums contain some Romano-British material. Intending visitors are advised to find out the opening times before making a special journey.

Aldborough Roman Museum, Aldborough, Boroughbridge, North Yorkshire. Telephone: Boroughbridge (090 12) 2768.

Ashmolean Museum of Art and Archaeology, Beaumont Street, Oxford OX1 2PH. Telephone: Oxford (0865) 278000.

Birmingham Museum and Art Gallery, Chamberlain Square, Birmingham B3 3DH. Telephone: 021-235 2834.

Bristol Museum and Art Gallery, Queens Road, Bristol BS8 1RL. Telephone: Bristol (0272) 299771.

British Museum, Great Russell Street, London WC1B 3DG. Telephone: 01-636 1555.

Calleva Museum, Rectory Grounds, Silchester Common, Silchester, Reading, Berkshire. Telephone: Silchester (0734) 700322.

Cambridge University Museum of Archaeology and Anthropology, Downing Street, Cambridge CB2 3DZ. Telephone: Cambridge (0223) 337733.

Carlisle Museum and Art Gallery, Tullie House, Castle Street, Carlisle, Cumbria CA3 8TP. Telephone: Carlisle (0228) 34781.

Chelmsford and Essex Museum, Oaklands Park, Moulsham Street, Chelmsford, Essex CM2 9AQ. Telephone: Chelmsford (0245) 353066.

Chichester District Museum, 29 Little London, Chichester, West Sussex PO19 1PB. Telephone: Chichester (0243) 784683.

Clifton Park Museum, Clifton Park, Rotherham, South Yorkshire S65 2AA. Telephone: Rotherham (0709) 382121.

Colchester and Essex Museum, The Castle, Colchester, Essex CO1 1TJ. Telephone: Colchester (0206) 712490.

Corbridge Roman Station, Corbridge, Northumberland. Telephone: Corbridge (043 471) 2349.

Corinium Museum, Park Street, Cirencester, Gloucestershire GL7 2BX. Telephone: Cirencester (0285) 5611.

Devizes Museum, 41 Long Street, Devizes, Wiltshire SN10 1NS. Telephone: Devizes (0380) 77369.

Dorset County Museum, High West Street, Dorchester, Dorset DT1 1XA. Telephone: Dorchester (0305) 62735.

Gloucester City Museum and Art Gallery, Brunswick Road, Gloucester GL1 1HP. Telephone: Gloucester (0452) 24131.

Grosvenor Museum, 27 Grosvenor Street, Chester, Cheshire CH1 2DN. Telephone: Chester (0244) 21616.

Housesteads Museum, Bardon Mill, Hexham, Northumberland. Telephone: Bardon Mill (049 84) 363.

Hull Transport and Archaeology Museum, 36 High Street, Hull, North Humberside. Telephone: Hull (0482) 222737.

Jewry Wall Museum, St Nicholas Circle, Leicester. Telephone: Leicester (0533) 544766.

Leeds City Museum, Municipal Buildings, Calverley Street, Leeds LS1 3AA. Telephone: Leeds (0532) 462632.

Legionary Museum, High Street, Caerleon, Gwent NP6 1AE. Telephone: Newport (0633) 423134.

Letocetum Museum, Wall, near Lichfield, Staffordshire. Telephone: Lichfield (0543) 480768.

Lincoln City and County Museum, Broadgate, Lincoln LN2 1HQ. Telephone: Lincoln (0522) 30401.

Museum of Antiquities, The Quadrangle, The University, Newcastle upon Tyne NE1 7RU. Telephone: Tyneside (091) 2328511 extension 3844.

Museum of London, London Wall, London EC2Y 5HN. Telephone: 01-600 3699.

National Museum of Wales - Main Building, Cathays Park, Cardiff, South Glamorgan CF1 3NP. Telephone: Cardiff (0222) 397951.

Newport Museum and Art Gallery, 5 John Frost Square, Newport, Gwent NP9 1HZ. Telephone: Newport (0633) 840064.

Nottingham University Museum, The University, Nottingham NG7 2RD. Telephone: Nottingham (0602) 506101.

Peterborough Museum and Art Gallery, Priestgate, Peterborough, Cambridgeshire PE1 1LF. Telephone: Peterborough (0733) 43329.

Reading Museum and Art Gallery, Blagrave Street, Reading, Berkshire RG1 1QH. Telephone: Reading (0734) 55911.

Roman Baths Museum, Abbey Churchard, Bath, Avon BA1 1LZ. Telephone: Bath (0225) 61111.

Roman Painted House, New Street, Dover, Kent. Telephone: Dover (0304) 203279.

Roman Palace, Salthill Road, Fishbourne, Chichester, West Sussex PO19 3QR. Telephone: Chichester (0243) 785859.

Rowley's House Museum, Barker Street, Shrewsbury, Shropshire SY1 1QT. Telephone: Shrewsbury (0743) 61196.

Royal Albert Memorial Museum, Queen Street, Exeter, Devon EX4 3RX. Telephone: Exeter (0392) 77888.

Royal Museum and Art Gallery, High Street, Canterbury, Kent CT1 2JE. Telephone: Canterbury (0227) 452747.

Royal Museum of Scotland, Queen Street, Edinburgh EH2 1JD. Telephone: 031-577 3550.

Salisbury and South Wiltshire Museum, The King's House, 65 The Close, Salisbury, Wiltshire SP1 2EN. Telephone: Salisbury (0722) 332151.

Scunthorpe Borough Museum and Art Gallery, Oswald Road, Scunthorpe, South Humberside DN15 7BD. Telephone: Scunthorpe (0724) 843533.

Somerset County Museum, Taunton Castle, Castle Green, Taunton, Somerset TA1 4AA. Telephone: Taunton (0823) 55504.

South Shields Museum and Art Gallery, Ocean Road, South Shields, Tyne and Wear NE33 2TA. Telephone: Tyneside (091) 4568740.

Stroud District Museum, Lansdown, Stroud, Gloucestershire GL5 1BB. Telephone: Stroud (045 36) 3394.

Verulamium Museum, St Michael's, St Albans, Hertfordshire AL3 4SW. Telephone: St Albans (0727) 54659, 59919 or 66100, extension 296.

Viroconium Museum, Wroxeter Roman Site, Wroxeter, Shrewsbury, Shropshire. Telephone: Cross Houses (074 375) 330.

Winchester City Museum, The Square, Winchester, Hampshire. Telephone: Winchester (0962) 68166, extension 269.

Yorkshire Museum, Museum Gardens, York YO1 2DR. Telephone: York (0904) 29745.

10
Further reading

Rodwell, W. and Rowley, T. (editors). *The Small Towns of Roman Britain*. British Archaeological Reports 15, 1975.

Miles, D. (editor). *The Romano-British Countryside*. British Archaeological Reports 103, 1982. (Especially N. Johnson and P. Rose on Cornish settlements).

Both of these academic reports are milestones in the study of the Romano-British countryside. They contain articles by many different people, concerning various areas. The second report was the successor to an earlier conference report which was also of great importance and which contains a number of interesting articles:

Thomas, C. (editor). *Rural Settlement in Roman Britain*. CBA, 1966. (Especially H. C. Bowen and P. J. Fowler on Dorset and Wiltshire and G. Jobey on the northern frontier settlements).

G. Jobey's pioneering work on the frontier villages can also be found in greater detail in *Archaeologia Aeliana* 42 (1964).

Site reports

Leech, R. *Excavations at Catsgore 1970-1973*. WAT, 1982.

Potter, T. 'The Roman Occupation of the Central Fenland', *Britannia* 12 (1981), pages 99-133.

Rawes, B. 'The Romano-British Site at Brockworth, Gloucs', *Britannia* 12 (1981), pages 45-77.

Rawes, B. 'The Romano-British Site on the Portway, near Gloucester', *Transactions of the Bristol and Gloucestershire Archaeological Society* 102 (1984), pages 23-73.

Wedlake, W. J. *Camerton*. Camerton Field Club, 1958.

For regional coverage consult the 'Peoples of Roman Britain' series, now published by Alan Sutton, for example:

Brannigan, K. *The Catuvellauni*. 1986.

Cunliffe, B. *The Regni*. 1973.

Detsicas, A. *The Cantiaci*. 1983.

Index

Page numbers in italic refer to illustrations